Edizioni PensareDiverso
Cenacolo Jung Pauli

George Anderson

Strange coincidences in your life.

Small curious events.
Forebodings. Telepathy.
Does it happen to you too?
Quantum physics and the theory
of synchronicity explain
extrasensory phenomena.

Summary

Prologue

From the earliest developments of thought, mankind believed that some significant coincidences were signs by which a higher philosophical or divine level sought to inter-dialogue with men.

In the last three centuries these convictions had been erased by new scientific tendencies. Extraordinary facts were considered as simple cases. Anyone who wanted to interpret extraordinary events as divine signals was destined for irony.

In the same way the visions of the future were considered illusions or even signs of imbalance. This happened despite the fact that many people had experienced these extraordinary facts.

Science denied the existence of a psychic dimension with which the human mind could interact. According to the common opinion, the only existing reality were material objects. However, in the 1980s, many experiments in quantum physics demonstrated the existence of a universe that is not just composed of matter. This universe contains a level in which energy and information do not suffer the limits of space and time typical of classical physics.

This confirms all the intuitions matured in the history of humanity. Among these intuitions the concept of "Soul of the World" enunciated by the Greek philosopher Plato. More recently, the Swiss psychologist Carl Gustav Jung has elaborated the theory of the "collective unconscious".

This book avoids investigating excessively specialized topics. The author clearly accompanies the reader in understanding the three levels that form a single reality.

The first level is the physical one, which is part of our daily experience. The second level is the one described by quantum physics, typical of the smallest elementary particles of atoms.

The third is the psychic level called "non-locality". It is the spiritual level, which can not be physically located anywhere.

This path of knowledge refers to recent discoveries recognized by official science. The strange coincidences and phenomena of the mind become important parts of a new and surprising reality.

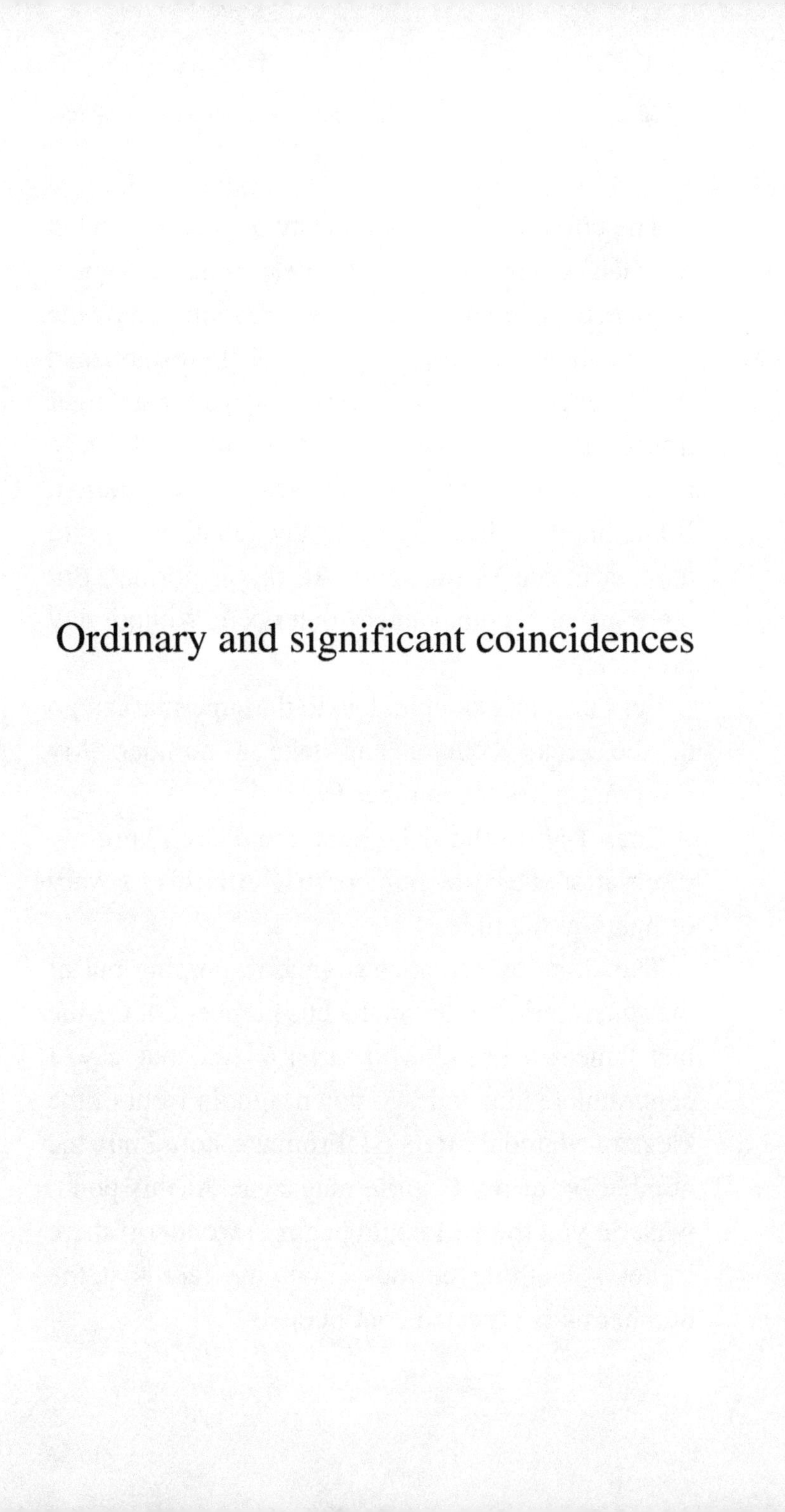

Ordinary and significant coincidences

The coincidence consists of two facts connected to each other in order to determine a logical sequence. A coincidence can be programmed by the will of men. A classic example of pre-established coincidences are the timetables for passenger transport lines. Depending on the scheduled times, a means of transport arrives at a station. Immediately after the journey continues with another means of transport. All this is normal. But there are also coincidences that occur without any predictions.

Let's take an example. I go to the supermarket, go to the bread counter and take a number. My reservation has the number 64.

Then I go to the fish counter and even here my reservation has the number 64. All this is very ordinary at the time.

The situation becomes strange if, coming out of the supermarket, I get on the bus number 64. On the bus I meet a friend who turns 64 on that day. I congratulate him and I go down right in front of the kiosk of Marconi Street 64. From the store I buy the number 64 of my favorite magazine. At this point, what do you think? I could begin to wonder if there is not something curious about the fact that the number 64 is repeated continuously.

To tell the truth, such numerical sequences happen with a certain frequency, but we do not notice it, because we are busy thinking about something else. Therefore, the coincidences linked to a number, similar to the one told, are strange but we do not take them into consideration. In fact, we do not notice these. These coincidences do not become "significant". Many coincidences could become significant if we became aware of them and started to make the brain work.

The question should be: what sense does this have for my life?

An old photo.

Mary was bored. That Sunday afternoon, due to a slight sprained ankle, she was forced to stay at home. After flipping through all her books he looked for an interesting TV program but did not find it. So she decided to do some useful little work. For example, there was a poster to hang. She had bought it a few months ago, and he was still well rolled up in its container.

This activity seemed to her too demanding. She decided on another small business. She decided it was the right time to change the lining made of paper in the drawer of her desk.

The drawer was wide and deep. Maria pulled it out, put it on the table and began to transfer all the contents into a box. As she picked up the individual items she was amazed at finding so many little things she had considered lost.

After emptying the drawer completely, Maria freed the old paper from the thumbtacks that held it and pressed it into her hand to throw it.

At that point she discovered a rectangle of paper that had slipped right under the covering. It was an old photo.

In that image Maria was able to see herself, much younger, together with some friends during a school trip that took place at least twenty years before.

Maria began to examine the photo with nostalgia because she recognized the reproduced people. Of course, the one on the left was Paolo, and the one next to him was Sergio, nicknamed "Lo Sguincio". The girl in the center was Arianna called "La micia". They were all friends that she was still seeing, but that guy between Laura and Silvio, the fat guy, who was he? He tried to remember and in the end was the lighting: but yes, it was Ciccio. By the end of high school his family had moved, so the contacts had faded until the two had lost sight of each other.

She remained absorbed for a long time, fantasizing about that period of her life: the school and friends she remembered. Now Ciccio suddenly appeared on that boring afternoon. She changed the lining paper of the drawer and put it back in place. Then here thoughts focused on something else ...

The following afternoon, as she completed some household chores, the telephone rang. Would you believe it? At the other end of the receiver a voice began to say:

"Hi, are you Maria? I hope you remember me, I'm Ciccio and we went to high school together. Yesterday, as I was thinking back to those times, I felt the desire to recontact old friends and the first number I found in my phonebook is yours ...

Two facts that are not connected to each other can create a "significant coincidence".

As is obvious, the mere finding of an old photo is just a curious fact. But the phone call that Maria receives the following day establishes an unexpected connection. For Maria the discovery of the hoto and the phone call have a "unitary sense". When Maria establishes that the two facts have a meaning, the two facts become a "significant coincidence".

We are all protsgonists of significant coincidences. At other times we can witness the curious coincidences. Unfortunately, even if at the beginning we are a bit surprised, we subsequently decide that it is a case.

We certainly think we have experienced a curious case, but still only a simple case. As a result, we store everything in some corner of the mind.

Jung had the merit of having been the first to study scientifically, the phenomenon of strange coincidences. He started from the observation that no one can deny their existence. Jung has also provided suitable tools for understanding when a coincidence can be considered significant, or "numinous", and therefore becomes synchronicity.

Of course it is not enough to distinguish between common coincidences and synchronistic coincidences. We can establish that random coincidences are part of our daily life and derive from the intertwining of our activities with the events of the world around us. The characteristic of common coincidences is that they do not involve or interest us because we consider these coincidences to be obvious.

Synchronic coincidences, on the other hand, open up a huge window on the panorama of the mystery. These coincidences make us enter into worlds whose existence we never even suspected.

Behind every synchronicity there are entire unknown universes to explore, and an immense wisdom from which to draw. Unfortunately, we have no eyes to understand these landscapes. Likewise, we do not know the language through which synchronicities try to communicate with us.

There are tuning problems between our mind and the mind from which the synchronicities descend in our favor.

A small statue flying from the window

Remigia, the old attendant of the church of the Holy Archangels, once again observed a girl. As always, the young woman stopped and knelt at the back of the church. His visits always took place when the church was empty, at a time when there were no religious services.

The girl was always very prayerful, and her sad expression could be seen. That day, however, Remigia saw a tear shining on her face. The attendant, because of her natural goodness but also of a certain curiosity, waited for her to get up. As he went out he approached her, trying to open a dialogue with her, to discover the reason for his suffering.

Through a cordial exchange of thoughts and common arguments he gathered his confidences. The girl, whose name was Sabina, was passing the time of youth, and would have liked very much to find a boyfriend to create a family. Unfortunately the dream was not realized.

Remigia comforted her and gave her the best advice. Then he remembered that among his roles as church attendant there was also the role of selling souvenirs.

So the woman thought it was time to finally get rid of a statue of the Angel Raffaele. This sacred object depicted one of the three Archangels, and had been exposed behind the glass in the cabinet of memories for many years, since no one had ever bought it.

"See Sabina" - Remigia said, as he led her to the souvenir window - "I suggest you pray the Angel Raphael every day, who is the protector of the betrothed and of married love. This plaster model is a copy of a silver original found in Naples. The Archangel Raphael is depicted together with a young man and a fish. The young man was called Tobia, and he had set out on a journey to marry a young woman named Sara, as established by his family.

Unfortunately, Sara was the slave of the demon Asmodeus, so every time she got married, her husband died on their wedding night. This misfortune had already happened seven times.

But Tobia did not know that he would be her eighth husband.

Fortunately, while traveling to reach Sara, Tobia was accompanied by the Angelo Raffaele.

Once on the bank of a river the two stopped to rest. Tobia went to the shore to drink, but was attacked by a large fish. Raffaele helped him and together they killed the fish. The angel told Tobia to open the belly of the fish and extract his liver; he ordered him to keep it because it would bring him luck.

Tobias arrived at his destination and prepared to celebrate the wedding, while Sara's father was already preparing the tomb for him too. But that time the tomb was useless.

With the protection of Raffaele, the two spouses spent the first night praying and did fumigation with the liver of the fish. In this way the demon failed to approach and was defeated. Sara was released from the curse and lived happily with Tobias ".

Remigia cocluses the story in this way:

"You too, dear Sabina, can rely on Raffaele. Keep this little statue in your house, and say a prayer for the Angel every day. You will see that he will come to your aid soon.

Think, Sabina, that still today in Naples on September 29th many girls go to visit the silver statue. As we say in the Neapolitan dialect, they go "*a vasà' o pesce 'e San Rafèle*". (to kiss the miraculous fish of St. Raphael).

Sabina, with great hope, bought the statue and placed it on a cabinet at home. Every day he recited his prayer. Time passed: a week, a month, three months ... but nothing happened.

The fourth month, in a moment of particular despair, took the statuette and looked at it with contempt, murmuring:

"But what a San Raffaele! Not even he helps me! "

Having said that, he threw the small statue out of the window.

After a few minutes he heard the bell of the front door ring. He opened and found himself in front of a distinguished gentleman. With a certain embarrassment, he told her:

"Excuse me, I saw this little statue fall from a window. If I'm not mistaken, it came from this apartment, so I thought I'd bring it back ".

Sabina, stunned, made him sit down and offered him a coffee. They talked about this and that. He learned that this kind gentleman was called Giulio, and he was single. They decided to meet again. Later they met assiduously, and eventually married.

Synchronicity.

In the story of Sabina, where does the coincidence begin? In other words, where does the series of coincidences begin? It start when Sabina decides to go to the church of the Holy Archangels every day? It start when Remigia, curious, listens to her confidences? Or does it begin many years before, when a statue was never sold? Or does the coincidence begin when Giulio passes under Sabina's window at the same time as the girl throws the little statue out?

They are many facts, unrelated and distant in time. However, if we consider these facts all together, we can see that they become the coherent parts of a story. That is, these facts become "significant" and therefore as a whole they build a "synchronicity".

The term "significant" means something that contains and expresses a meaning. A significant event constitutes a "sign of heaven". The significant event speaks, is eloquent, remarkable, relevant.

Jung uses also the term "numinous" which means: surrounded by a halo of sacredness. A numinous event inspires fear and reverence together.

In the story just narrated the content of sacredness does not derive from the fact that we speak of the statuette of a saint, or from the fact that the episode of Tobias is taken from the Holy Bible. The overall event of a synchronicity is "numinous" with a broader meaning. The fact is worthy of a particular respect because it is able to induce a subtle sense of spiritual fear.

Both of the two stories I presented, that of Maria and that of Sabina, can be considered synchronistic episodes.

In fact, their characteristics correspond to those indicated by Carl Jung to discern whether an episode is synchronistic or not.

According to Jung, the characteristics of a synchronicity are mainly three.

The first characteristic is that the two or more facts that make up synchronicity are not linked by a relationship of cause and effect. In the context of a synchronicity, none of the facts is a direct consequence of another fact. The connection is intellectual and occurs in the mind of the subject.

In the example related to Maria, it is evident that Ciccio's call is not the consequence of the rediscovery of the photo.

Similarly, the launch of the statue made by Sabina and the passage under Giulio's window are not consequent to one another.

The second characteristic of a synchronicity is that facts generate an emotional reaction in the person who is involved. In the first episode, Maria will remember history for years. In the second story Sabina is so pleasantly involved as to marry Giulio.

The third characteristic is the symbolic nature of the facts; unfortunately, this makes them difficult to understand. However, even when it is not possible to give a logical explanation as to why those events took place, one senses that they hide some mysterious message waiting to be deciphered. If we want to say it like Jung would, we say that "they have a numinous character".

Collective unconscious and
archetypes.

To fully understand the concept of synchronicity we need to examine Jung's theories. This examination will allow us to understand the origin and functioning of synchronicities. Jung uses a concept, already known in the evolution of human thought, and calls it "*collective unconscious*".

In his studies, Jung hypothesizes that the human psyche can be divided into three levels.

The level of individual consciousness

The first is the level we call "individual consciousness". This level includes everything we know about ourselves and the environment around us. The individual consciousness represents the ability to understand and evaluate the facts that occur in the sphere of our experience.

Thanks to our conscience we can reasonably foresee what will happen in our future, more or less close

The term "conscience" comes from the Latin "*conscire*", that is "*to be aware, to know*". In other words, consciousness indicates the awareness that each person has of himself and his mental contents.

Therefore conscience is the seat of our reasoning. In consciousness, decisions and behavior based on reason mature. The individual conscience operates discernment and makes reasonable choices, according to our way of understanding the world.

The individual unconscious

The second level is the place of the individual unconscious. Here are born and grow ideas, beliefs and behaviors that are not subject to our direct control.

For example, essential life functions like breathing and heart muscle contractions are performed here.

Furthermore, in the part of our consciousness that we do not know, the instincts, tendencies and attitudes inhabit. Among these there are also the "unconscious preferences" for a particular form of art rather than for another. The unconscious unconsciously determines the preference for one color or another, for a profession or another.

Sigmund Freud also referred to the personal unconscious. Freud teaches that this is an initially empty container, which then, in the course of life, is filled with all the "scraps of consciousness".

Jung thinks completely differently. He claims that the unconscious has its own functional autonomy from the beginning of the life of a human being. Indeed, according to Jung, man is governed more by his unconscious than by his conscience.

The subconscious would have a rebalancing function with respect to consciousness. There are contents of consciousness that can become unconscious; this happens in the mechanism of forgetting.

Furthermore, in consciousness there is information that can be forgotten voluntarily, because it is the result of painful events. Some experiences can be removed because they are connected to episodes of which we are ashamed or whose reality we want to deny.

In these cases a "removal, suppression" is carried out but it is never complete. In fact, all we do is move the memory from our conscious part to the unconscious.

In particular situations, however, experiences that seem erased can re-emerge from the unconscious.

The main difference between Freud's and Jung's thesis lies in the fact that according to Jung the subconscious is not just a warehouse that is progressively filled with experiences that are judged useless by conscience.

Jung values the subconscious much more positively.

According to Jung, the subconscious is a place full of new and creative ideas. In the subconscious many conceptual constructions and many original projects are born and grow, relating to the present and also to the future.

Therefore, according to Jung the individual unconscious contains seeds of knowledge and creativity. These are absolutely original ideas, those that would lead to formulating the classic questions: "But how do you know? But who told you that? "

The premise is this: the unconscious contains ideas that are not related to the experience of the individual; these ideas have always been present. From this premise comes "the question": if these ideas exist from before, *where do they come from?*

The collective unconscious

To better explain the collective unconscious we leave the word to Carl Jung himself, who describes it in his 1936 paper published with the title: "Das Konzept des kollektiven Unbewussten".

> "The collective unconscious is a part of the psyche. It can be distinguished from the personal unconscious by the fact that it does not owe its existence to personal experience and therefore is not a personal acquisition.
>
> The Individual unconscious is essentially made up of contents that were present in the consciousness, but then disappeared because they were forgotten or removed.
>
> Instead, the contents of the collective unconscious have never been present in consciousness and therefore have never been acquired individually, but owe their existence exclusively to inheritance.

The individual unconscious consists mainly of complexes. Instead, the content of the collective unconscious is essentially formed by archetypes.

My thesis, therefore, is the following. There is a first psychic system, which includes our individual consciousness. It also includes the personal unconscious. Beyond this, there is a second psychic system of a collective and universal nature, which does not refer to the individual sphere but is identical in all individuals.

This "collective unconscious" does not develop in individuals, but is inherited. The collective unconscious consists of "pre-existing forms", the archetypes. "

Therefore, according to Jung, there is a level of consciousness placed outside our mind, not confined to our skull but detached and autonomous with respect to our physicality.

This level of consciousness, being a psychic level, cannot be placed anywhere. It is not "a thing", it does not have width, height and weight. It cannot be taken from here and moved there.

The collective unconscious exists, in the same way that our soul exists. It exists as the age of a tree or the clarity of river water can exist. No one can see or weigh the age of the tree or the flow of the river, but no one can deny that they exist.

The collective unconscious is an absolutely psychic reality that contains the experiences of all human beings, in the form of archetypes. The advantage is that all human beings can "dialogue" with archetypes.

Today we can say, using a technological language, that all information relating to the human race is stored in an immense quantity of files called archetypes.

Since all human beings can interact with the archetypes of the collective unconscious, it follows that they all possess a great deal of knowledge, but they do not know it.

I write these words using my computer. In his memory there is a dictionary and a grammatical error correction program. I didn't create these supports and I didn't even know they existed until I made a mistake in writing.

I don't know exactly where these "applications" are. Perhaps they are placed "in the cloud". However, when I make a mistake, these applications intervene. The first few times I stood looking at the screen with the little words highlighted in red, and I didn't understand why. Gradually I got used to it and realized that the red underline indicates an error. Unfortunately, he often don't specify what error it is.

It would be interesting if the best parts of my writings appeared underlined in blue, to point out that some mysterious section of the software is satisfied for how I write.

Perhaps I would still not understand, because the computer expresses itself in forms that are not immediately understandable. It is often necessary to consult a reference manual.

Synchronicities are something like this. These are incoming signals to us from a "grammar checker" which is placed who knows where. It is a software dispersed in an immense "cloud", which speaks with us in "machine language", that is it expresses itself in a little decipherable way.

The archetypes resemble this grammar checker.

Sometimes the archetypes slide down from the collective unconscious and come to influence our consciousness. They come to suggest corrections on the lines we are writing in the story of our life.

We should avoid bothering ourselves when this happens, even if the intervention of the archetypes generates episodes that are difficult to understand, such as the strange coincidences. These are red or blue lines. We grasp the presence of a hidden meaning, but we do not understand its meaning precisely.

An idea as old as man

Carl Jung had the merit of exhibiting his thesis on the collective unconscious according to criteria of scientific rigor. However, the idea was not new. Since the dawn of humanity and since the first manifestations of human thought, the belief in a higher psychic level has developed. The concept of "world of ideas" was born in Greek civilization. In short, man has always believed in a spiritual domain that is disconnected from material reality, but usually dominates it.

Every time a divinity is identified in natural objects, such as the Sun or the Moon, a personality has always been attributed to that object. The Sun rises and sets every day to give life to the earth.

However, the Sun has a will of its own, so it may even decide not to arise. From this fear comes the need to it revere and it pay homage to the point of organizing a cult and offering sacrifices in order to please it.

The beliefs of the animist religions of the Paleolithic and the Neolithic period soon became, in the classical period of ancient Greece, in a more refined concept, that of the Soul of the world. Today this concept is known with an expression in Latin "Anima Mundi". It is a philosophical concept used by the followers of the Greek philosopher Plato to indicate the vitality of nature.

The Anima mundi expresses the totality of nature considering it similar to a single living organism. At the same time, however, the soul of the world is closely related to the soul of each individual. Thus the concept implies a universe in which "everything is one", but each individuality retains the characteristics that distinguish it.

In collaboration with Wolfgang Pauli (Nobel prize for physics in 1945) Jung deepened the possibility that the concepts of "Archetipo" and "Synchronicity" could be related to a reality that defined "Unus mundus".

It is a reality from which everything emerges and to which everything returns.

It is the same the concept of Anima mundi coming from the "monism" of Plato that was later and developed by the Neoplatonist philosophers.

The philosophies and religions have accepted and integrated the concept of the Soul of the world.

Today this concept is present, with different names, in Eastern philosophy. We can recall the "Tao" of Chinese culture, or "Ātman" of Indian culture. But we find this concept also in Western religiosity, in the figure of the "Holy Spirit".

The secular culture also refers to the Soul of the world with many different names such as, for example, universal Mind, Global Consciousness, Spirit of the world.

Speaking of the "collective unconscious" we do not refer to any of these Entities but we stress that there are strong similarities with each of them.

The archetypes

Thus, the collective unconscious evokes many similarities with the spiritual concepts elaborated in human cultural evolution.

Other similarities are evoked by another concept linked to the Jungian collective unconscious. Let's talk about the "archetypes".

The archetypes are conceptual categories considered similar to archaic structures like those typical of myths and religions, but also to the fairy-tale characters of popular culture.

Indeed, Jung himself believed that he had not proposed anything new, but he recognized that archetypes can be considered similar to the main mythological typologies of every historical era and of every human race.

Therefore, archetypes can be as infinite as the capacity of human thought to generate real or fantastic situations is infinite.

There is the archetype of death and the archetype of fear, the archetype of cruelty and the archetype of piety.

There are also all the archetypes connected to the visions generated by our dreams. In dreams dreamlike figures become symbols, that is, they become archetypes. Let's talk about figures like the horse, the spider, the leap into the void or the wolf that pursues us.

Any figure imagined by our mind is present as an archetype in the collective unconscious. Each figure has a meaning that does not correspond to the figure itself, but has a symbolic value. For example, the horse symbolizes the desire to travel in the spiritual worlds.

Plato also believes that archetypes are something that belongs to us by inheritance, without having experienced their contents directly.

The philosopher believes that we know the archetypes because we have already seen them before being born. To support this theory he uses the "doctrine of reminiscence". Our soul, before entering a body, is lived in the "World of Ideas". In this world it has acquired his knowledge; and preserves it when it is embodied in a body. Therefore Plato states that "to know is to remember" because we would have acquired knowledge before birth.

In contrast, Jung's collective unconscious is a place where ideas are not accessible to our soul before birth. These ideas, that is the archetypes, are manifested in our individual unconscious throughout our life.

Sometimes we consider archetypes as abstract concepts. Jung did not consider them as such, because abstractness does not have its own "form". Jung, on the other hand, believed that the archetypes were capable of assuming a "form" to manifest themselves.

Being able to "take forms" in our unconscious, archetypes are sources of "psychic energy", and are able to discharge their potential on human beings through dreams, strange coincidences, premonitions and spiritual insights that are the basis of synchronistic episodes.

The difference between Plato's conception and Jung's conception lies in the process by which we know the inherited ideas that are not related to the experience.

According to Plato the soul knows the ideas before going down into the body. According to Jung, instead, the archetypes interact with the individual unconscious only after birth and throughout life.

This difference becomes more evident if we consider that, according to Jung, the action of the archetypes becomes much more powerful at times when the individual goes through moments of stress or moments of crisis and transformation.

In fact, the conscious part of the individual is more rational and is more inclined to accept compromises with the reality of life.

Instead the subconscious is more instinctive and imaginative, and often does not fear to embark on instinctive and irrational behaviors.

As a result, the conscious part of the individual raises a solid projection barrier to keep the unconscious effervescence at bay.

This is not always good, and many times it doesn't work. There are times when the barrier raised by the consciousness wobbles or even collapses. They are moments of existential crisis, such as the loss of a job, or the end of a relationship, or the death of a loved one.

In these cases the rational conscience is upset, because it clashes with a reality that did not imagine so raw and painful. Conscience questions the correctness of its convictions and asks itself how it may have made a mistake.

In these cases the defenses are lowered, the protective barrier is no longer unbeatable.

Through the subconscious of the individual a flow of psychic materials is created that can take the form of synchronicity.

Therefore, normally, a synchronicity always accompanies the need for change. Sometimes it precedes it or proposes it. However, it always does it in a symbolic form, using an extremely difficult language to decipher.

Probably, among the examples present in Jung's archive, the most famous is that which occurred during the therapy of one of his patients. In his essay published in 1952 with the title " *Synchronicity: An Acausal Connecting Principle*" Jung describes the event with these words:

> "One patient had a dream at a decisive moment in the therapy. In the dream the young woman received a gold beetle as a gift. While she was telling me this dream, I was sitting with my back to the closed window.
>
> Suddenly I heard a noise behind me, as if something was knocking softly against the window.
>
> I turned and saw a winged insect that, from outside, bumped against the

window. I opened the window and caught the insect. It was very similar to a gold beetle, that is, to a "Cetonia aurata", the beetle of roses.

Evidently, the insect had felt impelled, at that very moment, to enter our dark room. This, contrary to his habits.

I must add that such a case had never happened to me before and it never happened to me afterwards; That dream of the patient remained a unique fact in my experience. "

Later Jung comments that the patient was an exceptionally difficult case. Until that day, she had not even had a small improvement. She was a very rational woman in her beliefs. An extraordinary event would have been necessary to shake she, but Jung could not produce it.

The dream of the scarab had had that function, because. she had impressed the patient, so she had begun to diminish her armor. However, when the beetle really came in through the window, the young girl had a much stronger reaction, which Jung describes as follows:

"Its natural essence succeeded in breaking the armor and the process of transformation that must always accompany a therapy, began to take off".

Later Jung explains the event in psychotherapeutic terms and describes why the episode proved to be effective for the patient's recovery.

Jung points out that the beetle is a classic symbol of rebirth. According to the description of the ancient Egyptian book "Am-Tuat", the Sun God, on his way after death, turns into a scarab at the tenth station.

In this form, the Sun ascends to the twelfth station. Here, rejuvenated, he can get on the boat that transports him to the dawn sky. In this way the Sun God can be reborn in a new day.

How synchronicity occurs

Synchronicities happen in people's lives, suddenly, when the ailing psyche perceives some analogy between his needs and the archetypes of the collective unconscious. In these cases the psyche accesses the archetypes through the subconscious.

Indeed, archetypes are eager to collaborate in the well-being of the individual. According to some theories the same archetypes have the ability to take the initiative.

The difference is substantial. In the first case the existence of a psychic container is assumed from which the information that has always been stored and is available to be used can be drawn.

In the second case, on the other hand, the existence of a superior Intelligence capable of knowing the needs of individuals and capable of intervening autonomously in their aid is prefigured.

In most cases the second hypothesis seems to be the most probable. Analyzing various cases of synchronicity, we would all be led to identify a direction, or even the presence of a "universal Spirit". We are talking about a "soul of the world" capable of making itself present and working in favor of all creatures, without limits of space and time. We can call this Spirit by the name we prefer.

In this way the universe becomes something interconnected (entangled) in all its parts. Each apparently separate element, in effect, constitutes a single thing with the whole.

Man, even in his individuality, that is, in his ego, becomes a molecule, part of a larger organism that we can call intelligent Cosmos. With his intelligence the Cosmic Mind (or Universal Mind) protects and guides him through synchronistic episodes.

Jung called this unifying reality of matter and mind as "*das Psychoide*". It is a level that is above matter and psyche, but includes both.

After all, as we saw in the previous examples, the collective unconscious looks nothing like a warehouse, but it has an intelligence extended to the past and the future. This intelligence cannot be explained by our categories of thought. We are used to a world where things happen one after another. In our experience every fact is "consequence" of a previous fact and "cause" of a subsequent fact.

At the level of the collective unconscious, information can reach consciousness in any order, without respecting the course of time. This happens when a premonition warns us of something before the fact happens. It also happens when a "telepathic call" tells us the dangerous situation of a person to whom we are bound by friendship bonds. In this case the communication has no time or distance limits. The person may be hundreds of miles away.

There are thousands of testimonies of people who have woken up in the middle of the night, while a friend is being attacked or involved in an accident.

There are also innumerable testimonies of the awareness, at the very moment when this happens, of the death of a person who lives far away.

We can summarize the typical characteristics of a synchronistic phenomenon in the few statements that follow.

A synchronicity is the sum of two or more main facts that are not logically linked together. These facts acquire meaning only for the person receiving the synchronicity.

Synchronicity occurs in two parts. The first part is this. Anywhere in the world and at any time a person receives an image in his unconscious. He can receive it in the form of a dream, a presentiment, a telepathic call, a sudden idea, a direct image or a symbolic image.

The second part is this: in any place in the world and at any time, an event or a real fact confirms the image received by the person.

Or the person who receives the synchronicity can interpret it as a guide to the improvement of his life.

Fate or synchronicity?

The American writer Louis L'Amour, (pseudonym of Louis Dearborn LaMoore) tells on his website the incredible story of Mrs. Sarah Richley, a quiet housewife. His son Peter had an overwhelming passion for the sea. Peter, as an adult, decided to embark and spend his life in the element he loved so much. He did so despite his mother's concern and contrary opinion. Both for the negligence and for the difficulties in maintaining contact with the mainland, mother and son lost sight of each other.

This is the prologue, after which the story takes place in two acts.

The first act will serve to retrace the adventure Peter lived in one of his trips, in 1829. These are facts that really happened, diligently reported in the naval registers. These incredible facts that were included in the seventh volume of the "Great encyclopedia of the sea" directed by the famous documentary filmmaker Folco Quilici.

The incredible story of Sarah Richley. Act I

In October 1829 the Australian schooner Mermaid sailed from Sydney to Collier Bay, in the western part of the Australian continent. n October 1829 the Australian schooner Mermaid sailed from Sydney to Collier Bay, in the western part of the Australian continent. La nave, sotto il comando di Samuel Nolbrow, aveva 18 uomini di equipaggio, tra cui Peter Richley, e trasportava anche tre passeggeri. . On the fourth day of navigation, when the boat was in the extremely dangerous Torres Strait, between Australia and New Guinea, the irreparable happened.

Banks of threatening clouds approached. The wind ceased and the ship was immobilized. In the middle of the night, a violent storm broke out that hit the ship. The schooner Mermaid was slammed repeatedly against a bank of corals and shattered despite the crew's desperate efforts. The 21 men abandoned the wreck and dived into the sea and swam to a rock. The captain, who arrived last, found that all 21 were safe.

The survivors spent three days and three nights on the rock. Finally, the Swiftsure brig which passed in the area sighted them and picked them up, then continued its course.

After five days, however, Swiftsure encountered a turbulent sea current and sank.

All the occupants quickly abandoned the ship. This time too everyone was saved. In fact, after a short time, he passed the "Governor Ready" schooner, with 32 crewmen. The schooner picked up and housed the survivors of the two previously sunk ships on board.

Unfortunately, the negative events were not yet over. The schooner resumed its journey but was weighed down by too many people.

Not many hours passed when a fire broke out on board. Perhaps the fire had been on with little prudence by the castaways.

No one managed to tame the flames and all the "Mermaid", "Swiftsure" and "Governor Ready" crews were forced to get on the lifeboats.

However, also this time the survivors could thank the good fortune because after a short time the Australian cutter called "Comet" appeared on the horizon.

By a fortunate coincidence this boat had been hijacked by a storm, so he encountered lifeboats.

When the sailors of the "Comet" learned that the people gathered were the survivors of three shipwrecks they regretted having saved them, thinking that they could bring bad luck to them too. However, by now they were on board.

On the ship a climate of great tension was born because the sailors of the "Comet" were convinced that those people were accompanied by an evil fate. They feared that the same fate would also affect the "Comet".

They were not wrong.

After five days of navigation, the Comet also suffered shipwreck. This time there were no lifeboats for everyone, so many remained in the water clinging to the remains of the sunken ship. They were forced to resist for 18 days, before being rescued by a steamer from the Australian postal service, called "Jupiter".

Incredibly, after four shipwrecks there was no victim among the castaways. Indeed, no one was even injured except for the small bruises that can be imagined.

Probably, in this whole affair Peter Richley had calmed his desire for sailing. But the story was not over yet. After a brief navigation, even the steamer "Jupiter" crashed into a rock and sank.

Fortunately, the "City of Leeds" passenger ship was passing near this last shipwreck. This ship saved all the survivors from the five shipwrecks, and brought them to safety in Sydney.

In this Australian city all the castaways could tell their adventure.

The narrator, on the "Encyclopedia of the sea" concludes his story with this comment:

> "A simple coincidence? Perhaps, but
> in cases like this it seems that there is a
> superior entity that handles the events.
> This entity removes events from
> chance, and directs them to conclusions
> that seem to adhere to human desires ... "

Here ends the story we have defined as "First Act".

However, as far as Peter Richley is concerned, the story is not finished.

Before he disembarked, while still aboard the ship "City of Leeds", Peter lived the second act of history. This second act, if possible, is even more incredible than the first act.

The incredible story of Sarah Richley. Act II

Let's go back to the story of the writer Louis L'Amour. This time everything happens aboard the passenger ship City of Leeds.

This ship, departing from the United Kingdom and bound for Sydney, was transporting passengers of various social backgrounds interested in reaching Australia for the most diverse reasons. Considering the considerable discomforts of travel on ships in the nineteenth century, travelers were mostly young and robust, who enjoyed good health.

Normally the doctor on board had no major problems in carrying out his work.

On this trip, however, the doctor found himself in great difficulty because of an old lady traveling alone.

At one point the old woman had collapsed under the weight of her years and her illnesses, and had been admitted to the hospital infirmary bed.

The doctor had asked her several times:

"But why did you, old lady, want to take this journey from England to Australia?"

Each time the woman replied that she hadn't heard from her son for years. Since she had recently learned that this son worked on ships along the Australian coastal routes, he had decided to embark to be able to find him.

Each time, in these dialogues, the old woman took a small portrait from her purse to show the boy's face to the doctor.

"This is my son. It would be enough for me to see him once only to die in peace. Help me, doctor. "

The doctor was a sensitive person and he wanted to help her, but he didn't know how to do it.

After one of these interviews, the doctor passed a check-up visit to some of the shipwrecked men collected at sea.

While he still had the image of his lost son in his eyes, he found himself facing a sailor whose features were quite similar.

The sailor had dark hair, a high forehead, an aquiline nose, thin lips and a pronounced chin. On a superficial examination, he might have looked like the portrait. Even the age of the sailor could correspond. Indeed, there was a good resemblance.

The doctor was struck by an idea.

Why not present this young man to the old lady, whose sight was no longer perfect? This benevolent deception would have allowed her to quietly conclude her life.

The doctor explained everything to the young man and asked him if he wanted to lend himself to play the role of son. But the young man did not want to know.

The doctor insisted saying:

"Basically you would only do a good work. You should just pretend for a few minutes to call you Peter. "

The young man began to give in.

"So I wouldn't lie, because my name is really Peter. But I would like to know more. Who exactly is this lady? "

"It's an English woman, a certain Sarah Richley."

Young Peter paled and a deep tremor shook his whole body, then exclaimed:

"But it's my mother!"

The old lady was really her mother.

The case produced the result that the two met because of five shipwrecks.

But did this really happen by accident, or had it been an incredible series of synchronicity?

For lovers of stories with a happy ending, we will say that the lady, after the joy of finding her son, recovered her health and lived for many years.

She no longer lost contact with Peter, but he continued to surf.

Several sources on the web document this story, for example:

http://tardis.wikia.com/wiki/Sarah_Richley

The Pentecostal pastor Philip Harrelson remembers every year this story, in his sermon on the occasion of Mother's Day. This habit is remembered on the pastor's website:

https://www.sermoncentral.com.

Some argue that the story is not true, because the events took place in 1829 while the City of Leeds ship was launched later.

Actually every sea is full of ships of the same name.

In addition to the "City of Leeds" of our history, another "City of Leeds" was launched in 1903, along with its twin "City of Bradford". Another ship was launched in 1950 under the name "City of

Ottawa", but was later renamed "City of Leeds" in 1971.

Two other cargo ships with the name "City of Leeds" were launched in 1908 and 1944.

Synchronicities are emanations of a universal Mind.

Is there conclusive proof that synchronicities are not illusions of our psyche? Can we reasonably argue that synchronicities come from a higher Mind?We find proof of this when we discover the existence of synchronistic episodes that involve more people in the construction of an event that affects only one of them.

A similar event is represented by the incredible sequence of facts that I have just proposed in the previous story. I would like to remind you that these are facts documented in the Naval Registers.

. But there is much more. Synchronicities do not intervene only in the lives of individuals or small groups of people. Indeed, these phenomena intervene to shape the collective destiny of the world.

Synchronicities guide communities of people, peoples, nations and the whole world towards a higher level of knowledge.

It is a path of cultural and spiritual evolution. Synchronicities guide humanity towards an unknown goal that can only be imagined.

The Jesuit scientist Pierre Teillard de Chardin theorized the existence of the "Omega Point".

This is the highest level of complexity and consciousness. I believe that A "Cosmic Mind" uses synchronicities to lead the human race to the "Omega Point".

Many people reflect on a strange peculiarity of the evolution of the human species. The man appeared about 4 million years ago. Since that time, man has lived for millions of years, in the brute state of the stone age.

In the last 12,000 years, on the other hand, man has experienced an incredible evolutionary leap that has transported him from the Stone Age to the Iron Age and then to the Information Age, the one we are currently experiencing.

Is it logical that for millions of years mankind has not achieved any significant evolutionary leap, other than that of the different stone processes, and then in a very short period it has reached the level of current civilization?

Only in the last 0,003% of its evolution has man been able to develop the new technologies that have transformed cities from aggregations of straw huts to expanses of skyscrapers.

It should be emphasized that the animals, while having the same time, did not realize any spiritual or behavioral evolution. A certain science that unites humans and animals does not know how to explain this fact.

If everything depended on man, we would have had to have a much more gradual evolution over time. But no, all our development, from the discovery of agriculture onwards, took place in a minimal part of our journey through history.

Is it possible to imagine that finally, after 99.997% of our journey, "Someone" or "some Energy" decided that it was the right time for humanity?

Someone, after four million years, finally decided that humanity had to be "pushed", "guided" towards a higher stage of its existence?

In the last three centuries we have experienced a period of profound materialism. At this time the existence of what cannot be weighed, measured and reproduced in the laboratory was denied.

Contrary to this materialistic tendency, many synchronicities, which are developing since the last century, want to lead the world to the awareness that the Cosmos is not composed solely of matter. Cosmos has two dimensions, the material and the psychic.

Many events of the last decades confirm this. We remember:

- The works of Carl Jung, a prestigious psychologist.

- The meeting and the collaboration of Jung with Wolfgang Pauli, Nobel prize for physics.

- The development of quantum physics and the discovery of the phenomenon of "entanglement" of which we speak in the second part of the book.

All these events and many other related events can be considered as part of a great synchronicity.

It is a synchronicity that is bringing down the false myths according to which the universe is made only of matter governed by chance.

At the same time, this global synchronicity predicts a new evolutionary leap of humanity. In this new level the reasons of the psyche, long repressed by materialism, will find their place and their importance.

All this is beautiful, but ... where are
the tests?

All that has been said so far has clashed, and continues to clash, with the absolutely majority part of scientific circles.

These environments deny, as a principle, the existence of anything that can be defined as "psychic" or "spiritual".

They claim that the whole universe is composed only of "things", that is, of matter. This materialist interpretation of modern science was born in the 18th century, with the advent of the Enlightenment.

The Enlightenment

The Enlightenment, which was born around 1700 in England, was a philosophical, political, cultural and social movement. This interpretation of reality developed rapidly throughout Europe and reached its peak in France.

The name "Enlightenment" derives from the will of its promoters and its adherents to "illuminate the mind" of other human beings who, in their opinion, were obscured in those days by superstition and ignorance.

The Enlightenment was embraced and adopted by most of the cultured and aristocratic society, despite bitter contrasts on the part of the ecclesiastical power.

But in the end the materialist vision succeeded in prevailing and oriented social customs towards its negationist values of the spirit.

From the early philosophers onwards it was considered that reason was a useful means of contemplating the truths. Instead, the followers of the Enlightenment considered reason as a practical, operational and functional tool for the development of mechanical progress.

According to the Enlightenment the conquests of reason are no longer in philosophical speculations, but in the achievement of practical results.

The Enlightenment argues that reason is useful only if it manages to explain facts and things with rationality, without referring to metaphysical arguments.

In the desire to free men from the unreasonable fears of the unknown, the Enlightenment claimed that every man possesses in himself the ability to understand the reality that surrounds him. However, to achieve this goal, man must free himself from superstitious beliefs.

According to the illumisti, these beliefs are imposed by a power interested in keeping the people in ignorance to be able to dominate it more easily.

The intentions were good. Unfortunately, in big revolutions the intentions are always, until one passes to their application. In practice it often happens that, after washing the baby, it is expected to throw it away with dirty water.

This tendency of the Enlightenment continues to cause damage in modern society

One of the cardinal principles of the Enlightenment states that the world is a machine. This machine follows the laws of physics known and those that are not yet known. Unfortunately, the machine has no purpose. There is no purpose in the whole of creation, and consequently there is no purpose in the existence of man. Man is also a machine that performs its vital functions without any purpose. When the machine breaks down, it ceases to exist.

Denis Diderot was the author, together with Jean-Baptiste D'Alembert, of the famous Encyclopaedia published in 17 volumes from 1751 to 1772. Diderot thus plays the role of a scientist:

> "The profession of the scientist is to
> instruct and not to give moral lessons. In
> his teachings he will leave aside the
> "why, "looking only at "how ".
> The "how" is derived from things,
> from beings. Instead, the "why" is only a
> fruit of the intellect. The intellect is not
> reliable. How many absurd ideas, how
> many false assumptions, how many
> chimerical notions are found in the songs
> in honor of the Creator!

Despite this rejection of all spirituality and the vision of a reality devoid of purpose and based on chance, the Enlightenment refused to be considered materialistic. The philosopher Voltaire repeated several times that he did not feel ready to decide either for materialism or for spiritualism.

The age of the lights and the literary salons

Precisely because of the expansion of the Enlightenment that began in the eighteenth century, that historical period took the name of "Siècle des Lumières".

Among the main protagonists we can remember the French Voltaire, Montesquieu and Fontanelle. But these protagonists acknowledged that they were inspired by English philosophy based on empirical reason and scientific knowledge, that is, on the predominant elements of the thought of Locke, Newton and Hume.

The Enlightenment received great help from literary salons.

This was a cultural tradition present in France since the days of Louis XIV. At that time there were ladies, known for their culture and their worldliness, who organized meetings in their living rooms, called "bureaux d'esprit". Sometimes the organizers were also men with a good social reputation.

Thus, the meetings of these "bureaux d'esprit" were organized by influential members of the upper middle class or aristocracy. These organizers invited celebrities to talk and discuss current topics. Among others, the parlor of Madame Geoffrin was well known. This lady invited literary and philosophical celebrities such as Diderot, Marivaux, Grimm, Helvétius.

With Madame Geoffrin the baron of Holbach competed, who organized meetings attended by the same characters already mentioned, in addition to the abbot Galiani and other philosophers.

Therefore, the substratum that nourished the Enlightenment consisted essentially of the aristocratic and high-bourgeois class. This circumstance makes us understand why the theories of the Enlightenment spread above all in the high levels of society.

Instead, in popular circles the diffusion was almost non-existent. As a result, those who should have been enlightened remained in the dark and were excluded from any benefit.

However, if we do not consider materialistic and atheistic positions, such as those of the last phase of Diderot's thought, the concept of "God" is found in most Enlightenment thinkers.

To reconcile this natural intuition with the theories they proclaimed, they tried to justify the existence of a God at the origin of the universe with scientific arguments. In this effort, considering the marvelous perfection of creation, they came to postulate the existence of a " eternal surveyor ". Voltaire also asked the question:

"When I evaluate the order and the prodigious ability of the mechanical and geometric laws that govern the universe, I am taken by admiration and respect.

I admit this supreme intelligence. I am convinced of his existence and I am not afraid that someone could change my opinion.

But where is this eternal surveyor? Does it exist in a specific place or is it spread everywhere? Does it occupy a space or not? I know nothing about this.
"

Unfortunately, Voltaire's doubts left no trace in later centuries. In the scientific panorama of today the concept of "God", even expressed in doubtful form, has been completely erased.

Today the scientific environments, with very rare exceptions, are oriented towards materialism, but fortunately they are not successful in spreading these theories.

In fact, human beings from all over the world, even those who have lived for long periods under the rule of atheistic totalitarianisms, continue to believe that they are not machines.

According to materialists uominins are random agglomerates of matter. It is excluded that men can possess a spirituality and a soul.

Strangely, materialists think that "others" are automatons without a critical sense, forced to behave according to mechanical laws. But they themselves are an exception because they are intelligent and can process autonomous thoughts.

What are the laws of classical physics that cannot be broken?

The denial of psychic realities derives from the fact that they are contrary to the physical laws on which the universe we know is based. Not only classical physics, but also the laws of relativistic physics are subject to these rules. These are clear and fully described rules.

The knowledge of these laws makes it possible to foresee at any time how the matter that makes up reality will behave. We can predict the behavior of objects, from our cigarette lighter to the farthest galaxy.

There is a criterion called "mechanicalness" that regulates the known universe. Every event depends on a cause. In turn, each fact becomes the cause that causes a subsequent event.

A moving object that hits an immobile object generates a thrust that can be calculated accurately.

In fact the thrust depends mainly on the weight of the two objects and on the speed of the first. The second object, in turn, moves in a direction that can be predicted. The speed and duration of the movement can also be foreseen.

Furthermore, everything in order to move has to have an "environment". For example, a ship moves over water and a car moves on the road. Music and voice propagate through the air, and are carried by sound waves.

Let's consider the three main laws.

The first law is the direction of time, also called the "arrow of time". Time only proceeds forward, and any fact that has already happened cannot be corrected or modified.

The chronological order of events is determined by the passage of time, which never allows us to turn back, even if sometimes an afterthought would be desirable.

The second law is speed. Nothing can move at a speed greater than that of light, equal to about 300,000 km per second.

The consequence of the third law is that any force decreases its power as a function of distance. This particularly affects gravity and magnetism.

For example, the force of gravity that attracts two planets decreases as the planets are distant.

The gravitational attraction of the Earth influences its satellite which is the Moon. However, the influence on Jupiter's satellites, like Europa or Ganymede, is absolutely inferior.

Likewise a magnet attracts an iron object placed at a certain distance: if, however, we move the object further away, the attraction diminishes and finally ceases.

The whole universe we experience obeys these laws. Therefore, we can understand the embarrassment of official science in the face of the possibility that something may escape these laws. Surely, among the things that do not obey the physical laws there are the extrasensory perceptions.

According to official science, the premonition cannot exist because it is not possible to know something first that will happen later.

Where could the information that underlies a premonition come from? There is no physical container in which information about facts that will happen in the future is stored. There is no archive of events that have not yet occurred.

Human thought is often mentioned, to say that it surely travels faster than light. Thought can explore both the past and the future. Thought can reach any area of our universe and other possible universes with the same intensity. This can be considered to be in conflict with the physical laws mentioned in the preceding paragraphs.

The answer of science is very simple. Thought is based in our brain and does not move from here. The thought does not come out of the skull. All mental elaborations are born and die within a few cubic centimeters of the physical brain. In practice, thought is illusion, not reality.

In this sense, premonitions are illusions that arise as waste products in the same brain. Even telepathic communications are not possible, because no thought can come from a head to fly into another head.

Therefore, to support the existence of a psychic reality like the one described in the first part of this book, it is necessary to discover a dimension of the universe in which the rules of classical physics are no longer valid.

This dimension should be similar to Jung's collective unconscious. If this psychic dimension exists, it can certainly accommodate Plato's ideas, as well as Jung's archetypes and any other non-material reality.

Until 1950 no scientist would have ever bet a single penny on this possibility. Instead, in the last decades there has been a big change.

Quantum physics has made great strides by investigating matter in the extremely small domain.

The possibility that an exclusively psychic dimension really existed was predicted already at the beginning of the last century. Finally, from the 1980s onwards, the existence of this dimension has been scientifically proven.

We are talking about the results of experiments on the phenomenon of quantum "entanglement".

Collaboration between science and psyche

A great synchronicity has been underway for several decades and affects the entire planet. This global synchronicity is leading humanity towards a completely different explanation of the reasons for our existence.

The universe is no longer a chaotic agglomeration of matter governed by chance. In this new vision the universe is an amalgam of matter and psyche, constructed in an orderly way and guided by a universal Mind.

This global synchronicity represents the sum of very many significant coincidences. Among these, there is certainly the meeting between the Swiss psychologist Carl Gustav Jung, and the Austrian scientist Wolfgang Pauli. We recall that Pauli will receive the Nobel Prize for Physics in 1945.

The two scientists met in Zurich, where they both lived. Carl Jung practiced the profession of psychotherapist. Instead, Pauli was Professor of Theoretical Physics at the Institute of Technology.

The meeting took place in 1932, at that time Pauli had asked Jung for an appointment to evaluate the possibility of undertaking an analytical therapy..

In fact Pauli asked Jung's help to solve some existential problems deriving from the human events in which he was involved.

First of all, Pauli suffered from his mother's suicide a few years earlier. Another reason for suffering was the new marriage of his father to a very young woman, the same age as Wolfgang.

Finally, another strong cause for suffering was the failure of his marriage to Kathe Deppner, a cabaret dancer. Unfortunately, this marriage lasted only a few weeks.

Consequently to all this, Pauli was going through a very difficult period of her life; these were the reasons that led him to ask for Jung's help.

However, immediately after becoming acquainted, a dialogue of a different kind developed between the two scientists. Jung gave the job of psychoanalytic therapy to a female doctor who was his collaborator.

Instead, the topic of the meetings between the two was their respective scientific knowledge. This relationship lasted for at least twenty-five years. When the two found themselves living in different places, personal encounters turned into an epistolary debate.

In their arguments, Jung and Pauli pushed to the limits of their respective fields of study, which were quantum physics and psychology. The two sought a link between the two sciences. In this way they bridged two fields of study that, until that time, were considered absolutely irreconcilable.

A cultural marriage was born between Jung's creativity and the rigor of Pauli's scientific discipline. With great patience the two confronted their theories without ever finding reasons for misunderstanding or breaking arguments. This happened despite the misunderstandings of the respective scientific environments.

Pauli approached Jung's thought and shared it seriously. In this way he overcame the prevailing mentality of the age, which defined the theories based on the psyche as "without any sense".

Pauli maintained a critical attitude, but he tried to understand Jungian theories.

Of course the main topic of the dialogue between Jung and Pauli was the relationship between physics and psychology, that is between psyche and matter. It is important to note that Pauli was not interested in synchronicity to satisfy a cultural curiosity. He believed he had been the protagonist of synchronistic episodes several times in his life.

In 1952 Jung and Pauli published a book together, *Naturerklarung und Psyche*. Both their agreement and their differences can be understood from the pages of this book.

Jung contributed to the work with his work entitled *Synchronicity: An Acausal Connecting Principle*

Pauli instead contributed with the essay *The Influence of Archetypal Ideas on the Scientific Theories of Kepler*

It must be said that Jung had long hesitated before publishing his ideas. It was Pauli himself who convinced him to publish them in this essay.

Overall, Pauli and Jung agreed that matter and psyche must be understood as complementary aspects of reality itself.

Reality is governed by archetypes, which must be understood as common principles of ordering. This implies that archetypes are elements that reside in a level placed beyond matter.

Pauli criticized the materialistic conviction present in his work environment. He did not share the denial of everything connected with spirituality, feelings and human emotions.

Pauli was convinced that in the near future it would no longer be possible to ignore the relationship between the external world of matter and the inner world of the psyche.

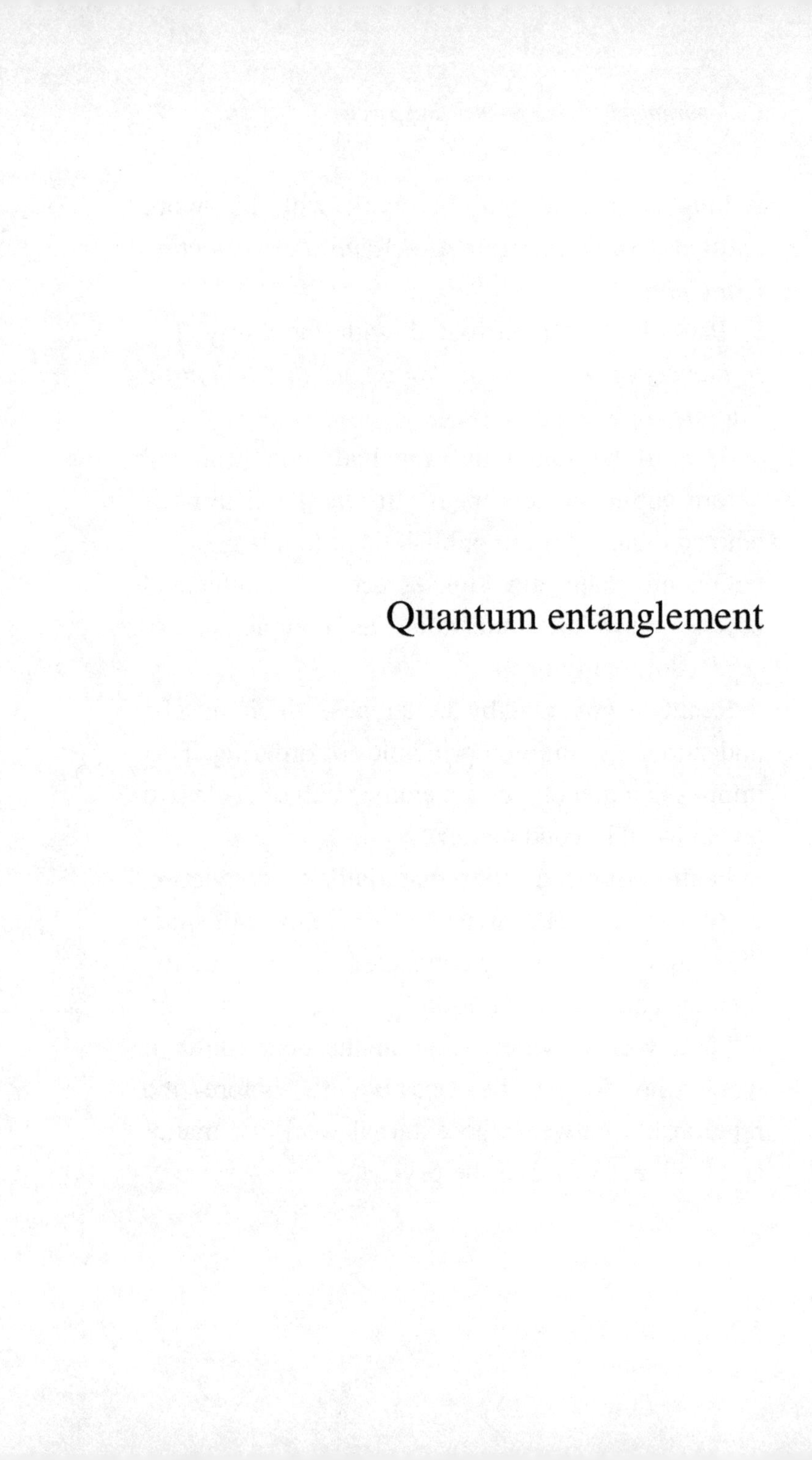

Quantum entanglement

The physical law called "conservation of energy" is one of the most important in nature. In its most studied form this law states that energy can be transformed and converted from one form to another. However, even if the shape of the energy changes, its total quantity does not change over time. We refer to the energy present in an "isolated system".

Of course, the universe is an isolated system.

Richard Feynman is an American physicist. He received the Nobel Prize for physics in 1965. In his book "The physics of Feynman, Vol.I" Feynman speaks thus of the law of conservation:

> "There is a law that governs known natural phenomena. This law has no exceptions, so, as far as we know, it is correct. The law is called "conservation of energy", and it is really a very abstract idea, because it is a mathematical principle.
>
> The law says that there is a numerical magnitude that does not change, whatever happens. His statement does not describe a mechanism, or something

concrete. This is a somewhat strange fact. We can calculate a certain number that represents the total energy of the universe. Then we look at things as they change. When we finish looking at the nature that plays its games, and recalculate the number, we find that it has not changed."

Without a doubt, we can take for granted that the overall energy of the universe can take different forms, but remains unchanged.

This law posed enormous problems when science began to study matter in the subatomic level, that is, the extremely small level.

We try to understand why.

Elementary particles are equipped with "spins". The "spin" is very similar to a rotational movement. Also the "spin" is subject to the conservation law.

So, if we take an electron with "spin" equal to zero and divide it into two parts, one part has "spin" +1/2 (positive half) and the other has "spin" -1/2 (negative half) . In this way the total of the two halves is always equal to zero as in the original electron. This means that the conservation law is respected.

Now let's do an experiment.

Let us assume that, after dividing an electron into two parts, we take a part and move it to any distance we can imagine.

Whatever the distance between the two parts, their "spin" does not change in order not to violate the conservation law.

But let's continue our experiment. , Let's take one of the two parts, for example the one with "positive half spin", and reverse its "spin" so that it becomes "half negative".

What happens at that point? It happens that the other half, wherever it is in the universe, also reverses its "spin".

The "spin" of the other half, which was "half negative", becomes "positive half". The two "spins" do not change "one after the other", but "at the same time".

It is important to understand that change takes place at exactly the same time. Information does not need time to become known to both halves.

With our experiment we reproduced the effect of the "related spins". Our two particles are said to be "correlated" because they were born together, when we split the original electron into two. The surprising news is that the related particles communicate with each other at any distance they are located.

If one particle changes, the other changes at the same time, because the energy conservation law cannot be violated.

The law of energy conservation cannot be violated even by a half electron, which is an absolute insignificant part of the universe.

If we tell it this way it may seem very little, but if we think about it, what we have just said *is in contrast with all the laws of classical physics*.

A violated rule is that relating to the speed of light, which could never be exceeded. In fact this speed is exceeded abundantly. As we have seen, we can place the two particles at any intergalactic distance, even at a billion light years from one another. Despite this distance, each particle reacts to the changes of the other in a contemporary way.

The rule of time direction is also violated. Based on this rule, each event occurs as a result of a previous event. In the case we have examined the two parts do not change their rotation according to a temporal sequence, first one and then the other, but simultaneously.

The concept of causality, according to which each event is caused by another event, ceases to be valid. This is also the consequence of contemporaneity.

Another principle that is not respected is the attenuation of the force fields, depending on the distance.

According to this principle the two parts should change with greater vigor when they are closer, and with decreasing vigor, as the distance increases.

Not so: the "bond of strength" that unites the two particles remains absolute and constant in space and time

The bond that unites the two particles takes the scientific name of "entanglement".

This term refers to the connection that arises between two particles created together, that is related.

This link has more spiritual than physical characteristics. Something similar often happens between human twins.

The most important observation was left for last and it is this: *how do two halves of the electron communicate with each other?*

It is obvious that when one of the two halves changes the sense of rotation, the news of the change does not cross any physical space and is not conveyed by any means.

If this happens, a time delay would occur. Yet action and reaction are contemporary.

There is no "time" in which information is still in the street, and the other part is waiting to receive it.

The information is both here and there. More simply we can say that information "exists" in an absolute way. Both particles possess it. The two halves of the electron share information as if they were still a whole electron.

The theory is scientifically confirmed.

The novelties of quantum physics were presented by Niels Bohr and his team of scientists, called "The Copenhagen School". This work group laid the foundations of quantum physics, in research conducted since 1927 onwards. Unfortunately, their insights were not very well received in the scientific world.

In particular, Albert Einstein judged this theory as impossible. He believed the basic reasoning was wrong.

According to Einstein the theory lacked a piece, which defined "the unknown variable". In practice, according to Einstein the calculations gave false results because there were some particular elements that were not considered. If he had added the so-called "unknown variable" to the equations, Niels Bohr would have obtained results closer to classical physics. Einstein was particularly concerned because Bohr's quantum theory was also in contrast with the theory of relativity.

Some scientists mocked Bohr's insights.

Yet Einstein, though convinced of his arguments, was too clever to deny a scientific theory before this theory was accurately evaluated.

He continued to argue that there was an error in Bohr's equations. But he had no prejudices and wanted to see clearly. Here is his greatness.

In 1935 he proposed a famous experiment, known as the EPR experiment. The acronym is born from the name of the three proponents, that is, besides Einstein, Podolski and Rosen.

The EPR was a "Gedankenexperiment" that is a thought experiment. In practice, it was not an experiment based on laboratory instruments, but on the reasoning and theoretical application of the known laws. This type of experiment, even if it is theoretical, can provide reliable results.

Mental experiments are still used today when the technical or economic means to carry them out in the laboratory are lacking.

Indeed, the development of the EPR experiment raised doubts about the credibility of quantum theories. This also depended on the complication of the executive protocol.

As a result, the scientific community took note of the results but did not consider them final.

Many years later, in 1964, another scientist again became interested in the issue.

John Stewart Bell published an article in which he proposed a simplified version of the EPR experiment. In the same article Bell proposed a practical method to carry out the experiment in the laboratory and invited the scientific community to implement it.

The invitation was collected by Alain Aspect, a French experimental physicist.

In the years from 1980 to 1982 Alain Aspect carried out the experiment in the laboratory.

In practice he proceeded by exciting an electron in order to force him to perform a double quantum jump.

The excited electron, in the double jump, emitted two elementary particles, that is two photons. Of course, the two photons were "related", as they were born in the same event.

Aspect's two photons generated in the laboratory behaved just as described in Bohr's theory. That is, the two photons have repeated the behavior of the two halves of electron I described earlier. This means that they violated all the rules of classical physics.

In the following years the experiment was repeated and confirmed many times by many scholars.

Today the laboratories no longer experiment the "entanglement" of two particles. In modern laboratories thousands or millions of related particles are created in a single event.

The dimension that goes beyond the matter.

In the light of current scientific knowledge, we can assume that communication at the level of elementary particles occurs with a method that is absolutely independent of matter.

The particles communicate in a level where time and space do not exercise their power. In this level two or more related particles, even if they are separated by infinite distances, behave as if they were one.

The Space", or the level at which this occurs, is called "non-locality". It is a psychic "space", because it cannot be placed anywhere.

Science reluctantly notes the existence of this space, since it cannot weigh it or measure it or reproduce it in the laboratory.

However, if this space exists, then other concepts of human thought can also find their place within it.

For example, we have previously cited the "collective unconscious" of Carl Jung or the "Soul of the world" by Plato. Subatomic particles act in the non-local, and no one can deny that this happens. Similarly, the psychic insights of human thought also become worthy of study and consideration.

Some might argue that the phenomenon of "entanglement" occurs only between the particles that have been related to each other in the laboratory.

We can remind these skeptics that the whole universe was born of a great laboratory.

We can imagine the initial universe as a "place" in which a great, unique explosion occurred, known as the Big Bang.

This explosion gave rise to all the matter in the universe. Therefore, all the matter of the universe was born from the same event.

This means that all the matter in the universe is related and constitutes a unique reality. Animals, plants and minerals are made of related atoms. The planets, constellations and the whole cosmos are related. Carl Jung and Wolfgang Pauli defined this reality "Unus mundus".

What role do coincidences play in my life?

At this point, each reader can legitimately formulate this question and can wait for an answer. We know that significant coincidences happen. Unfortunately, until today we have considered coincidences as bizarre and sometimes mysterious facts, but without importance in our daily life.

Significant coincidences can be defined more precisely with the name of "synchronicity". With this name we indicate the clues that attempt to explain the messages and intentions of a "Mind of the world".

Every synchronicity contains a message directed to us, useful to guide us in inner growth. Unfortunately, the language of these messages is symbolic. We struggle to tune into the right wavelength to decipher the contents of these messages. A quote from the American physicist Joseph Henry can help us understand the concept:

"The seeds of every great discovery are constantly present in the air that surrounds us, but they fall and take root only in prepared minds."

We are used to attributing unusual facts to chance. When coincidences are negative we attribute them to destiny, whereas when they are positive we attribute them to luck.

We quote a few other famous sentences. Arthur Schopenhauer said:

> *"Destiny shuffles the cards and we play."*

Instead, Louis Pasteur spoke thus of luck:

> *"Fortune favors prepared minds"*

These statements imply that every opportunity, mixed with a dose of preparation, can help us build a better life.

The preparation consists in knowing how to pick up, at appropriate times, the driving signals, in the same way that we know how to read road signs, while we drive our car.

Synchronicities are guiding signs, indicators that symbolically show us a direction.

It is difficult to understand the symbolic messages that come from the spiritual dimension, because we live deeply immersed in the physical dimension.

Moreover, as already mentioned, the synchronicities are constructions made of events disconnected from each other. These events have no cause and effect ties, and are distributed in space and time, so it is difficult to relate them.

The coincidences become meaningful only when we succeed in attributing a meaning.

We often need to use an irrational mental process to link certain facts between themselves.

In many cases it is necessary to ignore the daily logic of temporality, according to which some things happen before and others after. In synchronicities this does not matter and facts can be placed anywhere in the time scale.

The meaning that we attribute to synchronicities is generated on a spiritual level.

Consequently, if we want to understand why we have given special meaning to any of the facts we must investigate into the depth of our spirit. The interpretation elaborated by our spirit is always illuminated by the symbologies we possess.

The symbolism of the synchronicities we receive are always connected to the symbologies present in our psyche.

We own the interpretative key to the synchronicities we receive. This key is present in our consciousness or in our unconscious.

Synchronicities are archetypal symbols. They cannot manifest themselves in a completely unknown symbolic form. When a person receives a synchronicity in a symbolic form, that symbol has already passed from the collective unconscious to the individual unconscious.

The symbologies evoked by synchronicities are not indecipherable because they are already present, rooted and intertwined in our unconscious.

Deciphering synchronicities.

The synchronicities have specific characteristics whereby the deciphering of the message is possible almost exclusively for those who receive them.

These characteristics are the symbolic character and the close link with the individual's unconscious.

The methodology of professional therapists may be an exception. They are able to deepen the layers of deep consciousness, that is, those that not even the same subject can explore objectively.

In most cases, no one turns to a psychotherapist for help in revealing the symbolism of synchronistic messages. Consequently, we can give here some rough advice that can help the interpretation.

The first piece of advice is obvious.

Never consider significant coincidences as the result of chance. They can be messages from a "higher Mind". This "Mind" coordinates the harmony of the universe and wants to help us maintain our harmony. It wants to make us beneficiaries of inner well-being.

The second piece of advice is to rely primarily on one's own judgment. Our judgment is certainly the most qualified and the most informed to guide our interiority in the elaboration of the meaning of the symbols. Coime already mentioned, each has the interpretative keys of the symbologies he receives.

The symbols are the heritage of all humanity but, at the same time, they are closely conformed to our

"Selbst", to our culture and to our way of seeing the world.

We can say that the symbol is like the tip of a finger. There are billions of fingers, but at the same time we don't find two equal ones. Each has its own fingerprints that are unique and unmistakable.

The third piece of advice consists in not being in a hurry to attribute meanings.

Often a synchronicity is made up of multiple events distributed over time. We must create a secret drawer in our mind in which we deposit the messages we do not understand.

Every time we receive a new message we must compare it with all those that we have not yet solved. This practice can give surprising results.

If we quickly erase from our mind every curious coincidence, we risk interrupting a path. Perhaps the canceled coincidence was an important link.

In fact, a synchronicity can be explained through days or months, or even years, and any new significant coincidence can be the completion of a previous coincidence.

The place from which the synchronicities come is often referred to as "non-locality", because it is not possible to place it either in space or in time. There is no space or time in the non-local level. This is scientifically proven by quantum physics and the recent discovery of the phenomenon called "entanglement", which I described in its essential elements.

As an appendix to this third council, I provide another indication.

Many scholars and authors support the usefulness of keeping a diary of coincidences. In this diary we can also note the significant dreams, that is those that struck us most. Dreams can be synchronic, or prophetic. This is especially true when the dreamed event really takes place. These are rare cases, because even dreams are based on symbologies. It is possible to give meaning to an event by connecting it to a dream.

The three levels of reality

From what has been shown in the previous chapters, a representation of the universe emerges that is very different from the one we have been used to considering.

Of course, we all continue to see the world as we have always seen it. This happens because the five senses that nature has given us are tailored to experience this world.

The vital needs and the needs of survival mean that we can see, touch, smell, hear and savor reality in the dimension that conforms to ourselves.

in fact, our senses are not effective outside our dimension. We cannot explore distant galaxies with our sight. Our eyes cannot observe the movements of microbes.

We do not perceive the smell of the explosion of supernovae nor the color of the molecules that make up the various bodies.

Moreover, these functions go beyond our basic needs. Evolution has made us specialized only for what is indispensable to our existence.

Most frequencies produce colors and sounds that are not visible or audible to us.

The sense of touch and the sense of taste, as far as we can consider them refined, allow us to clearly distinguish only a narrow range of flavors and smells.

We can say that our five senses are very coarse and very limited tools compared to the infinite variations produced by the universe.

However, we also have two other senses. The sixth sense is intuition, which allows us to process very useful information in simple daily life, even if these informations are not essential for survival.

Intuition is a wonderful tool, which processes our experiences and provides advice on behavior.

The first men could guess the edibility of the berries or the danger of insect bites, evaluating their color or the shape of their body. On the basis of a summary examination of appearances they were able to calculate the greater or lesser possibility of risk.

Today we use intuition to evaluate people and occasions. Often, thanks to intuition, we are able to mature a spontaneous distrust towards those who would like to deceive us. So we can also guess who could help us.

Intuition helps us to discern the positive and negative sides related to a certain business. Intuition usually plays a decisive role in our decisions. Surely the intuto is an imperfect tool, but the experience helps us to improve it.

The sixth sense, or intuition, is based solely on thought, but it has nothing mysterious about it. the information we use to formulate our judgments is all contained in our memory and in our cultural baggage. The whole intuitive process takes place within our psyche. Intuition does not use knowledge beyond what we already have. Naturally, intuition is consistent with the world outside the psyche, that is, with physical reality.

The quantum level and the non-local level

We can define the "physical level" the environment in which we live. The physical level is made of solid objects and separated from each other. This level also includes the extremely large part of the cosmos, such as the planets and constellations. Today science tells us that there are at least two other levels. Although we cannot understand these levels with our limited senses, they nevertheless exist. Their existence is confirmed beyond any doubt.

The second level is quantum. This is a "space" in which elementary particles move and operate freely. These particles are not subject to any of the constraints affecting the macroscopic level of matter. As we have seen, the particles establish reciprocal bonds without limits of space and time.

This characteristic suggests the existence of a third level, that of non-locality, which is not made of matter. The non-locality contains only energy and information.

Non-locality is the level where the whole universe is connected and forms a universal "entanglement". The non-locality contains all the information, that is all the cosmic intelligence gained from the first moment of creation.

This information is supported by an unknown and unlimited energy, which distributes it wherever it is needed.

The seventh sense

If we want to access the non-local reality the five senses cannot help us. Not even intuition can help us. We need the seventh sense.

The sixth sense comes to our rescue by processing only the information we have accumulated in our daily experience,

Instead, the seventh sense allows us to come into contact with an immensely richer deposit, which contains all the experience of the universe.

From this deposit the presentiments, the premonitions, and the whole range of phenomena we call extrasensory descend into our consciousness.

The level of non-locality has always been known by every civilization, by every philosophy and by every religion. Unfortunately, it was not possible to prove his existence. Today, finally, the evidence exists.

We can be sure that an intelligence oversees the functioning of the non-local level. In fact, how could it be governed by chance?

From this level we receive messages. In most cases these messages are symbolic and we struggle to decipher them. However, it is possible that in the future humanity will be able to develop a more advanced understanding plan than the current one.

Each can call the level of the non-locality with the name you prefer. We can mention many expressions: Universal Mind, Global Mind, World of Ideas, Mind of the Universe, Collective Unconscious, Non-Locality, Tao, Atman, God, Holy Spirit.

We know it exists, and we know that from this "Superior entity" there are useful aids for the growth of individuals and the development of the whole human race.

We have called these aids "significant coincidences" and "synchronicity", referring to Jungian theories. However, everyone can call these interventions with the name they prefer: inspirations, prophecies, revelations, miracles, or whatever.

Maybe we will never be able to reveal in detail the mysteries we talked about. But there is an important novelty. In the past we referred to suggestive hypotheses, of which we could not provide evidence. Today we talk with confidence and confidence about a spiritual or psychic level, which actually exists.

Bibliography

Amir Dan Aczel, Entanglement. The greatest mystery of physics.

Barbour Julian, End of the time.

Barrow John David, From zero to infinity. The great story of Nothing.

Barrow John David, The numbers of the universe,

Barrow John David, Why is the world a mathematician?

Barrow John David, look Frank The anthropic principle.

Beitman Bernard, Messages from coincidences.

Cambray Joseph, Synchronicity. Nature and Psyche In a connected universe.

Cantalupi Tiziano, Santarcangelo Donato, Psychism and reality. .

Capra Fritjof, The Tao of physics.

John Cederquist, Coincidences They don't exist.

Cesati Cassin Marco, We're not here by chance.. The power of coincidences.

Subrahmanyan Chandrasekhar, Truth and Beauty. The reasons for aesthetics in science.

Chinnici Giorgio, Case Guard. The secret mechanisms of the quantum world

Chopra Deepak, Coincidences

Ford Kenneth, The world of Quanta. Quantum physics For everyone.

Gamow George, The Adventures of Mr. Tompkins.

Gamow George, Mr. Tompkins ' New World.

Goswami Arneb, Quantum Lighting Guide.

Greene Brian, The plot of the cosmos. Space,

Greene Brian, The hidden universes of parallel reality And the profound laws of the cosmos.

Greene Brian, The elegant universe. Superstrings, hidden dimensions and the pursuit of definitive theory.

Hawking Stephen The Universe in a nutshell.

Hawking Stephen The theory completely. Origin and destination Dell Universe.

Hawking Stephen The great history of the time.

Hawking Stephen Do Big Bang For black holes. A brief history of the universe.

Heckler, Richard, Coincidences.

Robert Hopke, Nothing happens by chance.

Joseph Frank, The power of coincidences.

Young Carl The analysis of Dreams. Archetypes of the unconscious. Synchronicity.

Young Carl Memories, DreamsReflections.

Kane Gordon, The Garden of Particles Elemental.

Shani Mani Quantum. From Einstein In Bohr, quantum theory, a new idea of reality..

Rei Hans, Christianity and Chinese religiosity.

Lederman Leon, Hill Christopher, Physical Quantum for Poets

Licata Ignazio, Watching the Sphinx.

Motterlini Matteo, Mental traps.

Peat David, Synchronicity. A union between the matter e Psyche.

Popper Karl, The Ego and your brain.

Radin Dean. Intertwined minds. Psychic phenomena explained by quantum physics.

Rhine Louisa, Psychokinesis. in mind Dominates matter..

Schumacher Ernst, A guide to the Perplexed, the B

Sheldrake Rupert, The illusions of Science.

Sheldrake Rupert, The mind Extended..

Michael Smith, Young and Shamanism.

Sparzani and Panepucci. (Curators) Young and Pauli. The original correspondence: The meeting between psyche and matter.

Henry Stapp Quantum theory and free will..

Michael Talbot, All is a. Feltrinelli

Teodorani Massimo, Bohm. The Physics of Infinity.

Teodorani Massimo, in mind Creative. From the physical universe to intelligent life.

Teodorani Massimo, The entanglement. The Weave In the quantum world: particles To consciousness.

Teodorani Massimo, Synchronicity. The link between physics and psyche. Da Pauli Young ' s Next In Chopra.

Teodorani Massimo, The Atom and the particles Elementary.

Seems Frank The physics of Immortality.

John White, The encounter between science and spirit..

Claudio Widmann, Synchronicity and coincidences Significant.

Claudio Widmann, Introduction to Synchronicity.

Finished printing on April 15, 2022

George Anderson is the pseudonym of Bruno Del Medico, blogger, writer, editor, specialized in the dissemination of issues related to social current events and the new frontiers of science. He is the author of many books on the recent Covid19 pandemic and of a series dedicated to quantum physics and metaphysics.